How do birds fly?

Disney BOOKS BY MAIL

When Mickey Wonders Why, he searches out
the answers with a little
help from these friendly experts:

Vice President and Publisher Cathryn Clark Girard
Director, Product Development Kristina Jorgensen
Editorial Director Lisa Ann Marsoli

DK Direct Limited

Managing Art Editor Eljay Crompton
Senior Editor Rosemary McCormick
Writer Alexandra Parsons
Illustrators The Alvin White Studios and Richard Manning
Designers Amanda Barlow, Wayne Blades, Veneta Bullen,
Richard Clemson, Sarah Goodwin, Diane Klein, Sonia Whillock

Contents

Why can monkeys swing from trees?

Because they have long arms and legs with strong fingers and toes for holding on to things. They also have a fifth toe that works like a thumb, to make holding and swinging even easier. But, that's not all! Some monkeys have tails that can curl around branches and grip.

A tale of two tails
Titi monkeys like company. At night they often wrap their tails together when they cuddle up.

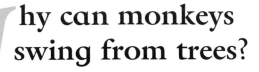

Bringing up baby
A baby monkey lives with its mother for several years. It clings to its mom's fur and goes everywhere with her.

Monkey business

Like people, some types of monkeys like to live in family groups.

Monkeys spend hours picking bugs out of each other's fur.

Yes, monkeys DO like bananas, but they will eat a lot of other things, too, such as insects, honey, and leaves.

Why do ducks waddle?

Because their legs and feet are really made for swimming, not walking. Their short little legs are at the back of their fat, round bodies. When they're in the water, their legs work like paddles and so they are very speedy and graceful. But when they're on land, their short legs and round bodies make them waddle from side to side.

Dipping and diving

Some ducks stick their tails in the air
and dip their heads just below the
surface of the water when they look
for food. Others dive down to the
riverbed for a mouthful of weeds
and a tadpole or two.

Duck! Here come the facts!

☞ Water birds have oily feathers to keep
them dry. The oil makes the water roll
right off them.

☞ Ducks have soft, fluffy feathers near
their skin to trap air to keep them
warm. These are the kind of feathers
that are used in comforters and quilts.

Why do frogs have such long legs?

On land, frogs' long back legs help them hop and climb – and leap away from enemies. In the water, their legs are good at kicking, making frogs speedy swimmers.

Frogmen
Divers who swim under water with rubber suits and big flippers are sometimes called frogmen.

The little tree frog

Here's a little frog that stays out of the water. It's called a red-eyed tree frog. It lives most of its life up in the trees. Its legs are very long so it can jump from leaf to leaf.

Drink up!
What's a frog's favorite drink?
Croaka cola!

9

Froggy foot facts

Frog's feet are shaped to help them do the things they need to do. Frogs that climb trees have feet with sticky pads to hold on with. Frogs that dig have pointed toes to shovel dirt, and frogs that do a lot of swimming have webbed feet to use like oars.

How do birds fly?

With the help of their wings, feathers, bones, and strong chest-muscles. Their feathered wings are strong, but light and bendable. Their bones are hollow, and their tail helps them balance and steer. When it flies, a bird flaps its wings down and forward, then more quickly up and back.

And now for something silly!
Some birds can't fly at all – like kiwis. They're just not designed for flying.

Flap, flap
What bird is always out of breath?
A puffin!

11

Dive bomb!
Kingfishers are very good divers. When they spot a tasty fish, their wings go back, their legs tuck in, and down they zoom, beak-first.

Flying facts

There are three ways of flying – flapping, gliding, and hovering. All birds flap their wings for take-off. Gliding birds hold their wings out and find winds to carry them along. Hovering birds flap their wings so fast they stay up in the air but don't move forward.

How does an octopus get around?

When it wants to go fast, it sucks water in to its body, then forces it out again – whoosh! The force of the water, as it is released, pushes the octopus along very quickly! When it wants to move more slowly, it uses its arms to swim or crawl along the ocean floor.

Speedy squid
Squid come from the same family as the octopus and they move in the same way. They are much speedier than octopuses though, and they sometimes shoot right out of the water!

Take that!
Octopuses can shoot ink out of their bodies. They do this to confuse their enemies, and so they can hide behind their inky screen.

Loads of legs
What is an octopus?
**A cat with
eight legs!**

13

Arms and more arms

People used to think that
octopuses were sea
monsters.

Octopuses and squid are
related to snails and clams.

What is the fastest animal in the world?

It all depends on the race. If there were a flying race, the spine-tailed swift would win. If there were a running race, the cheetah would win, and if there were a swimming race, the sailfish would win.

Look out below!
You'd have to give a special medal to the Peregrine falcon, too. It doesn't get its medal for flying, but for diving head-first down through the sky at more than 200 mph!

Race results

The swift can fly at a speed of 106 mph. The cheetah can run as fast as 63 mph. The sailfish can zip through water at an amazing 68 mph. To give you an idea just how speedy they all are, a super athlete can run around 20 mph!

Why do turtles walk so slowly?

Because they don't need to go any faster to escape danger! Turtles and tortoises carry all the protection they need around on their backs. They can pull in their head and tail, tuck their stumpy little legs under their bodies, and hide safely inside their bony shells.

16

Big turtle
One of the world's biggest turtles is the Galapagos turtle. It is a land turtle which can grow up to four feet long.

Hurry up!

Mother sea turtles lay their eggs in the sand. After the baby turtles have hatched out of their eggs, they head to the sea to begin their turtle lives.

Slow-moving facts

☞ The green turtle lives in the sea. It has paddle-like flippers to get around.

☞ Part of a turtle's shell is made of keratin. That's what your fingernails are made of, too!

How do flies walk on ceilings?

They've got little suction cups on their feet so they can walk on surfaces like walls and ceilings. The suction cups also release a liquid which gives them extra help to hold on tight.

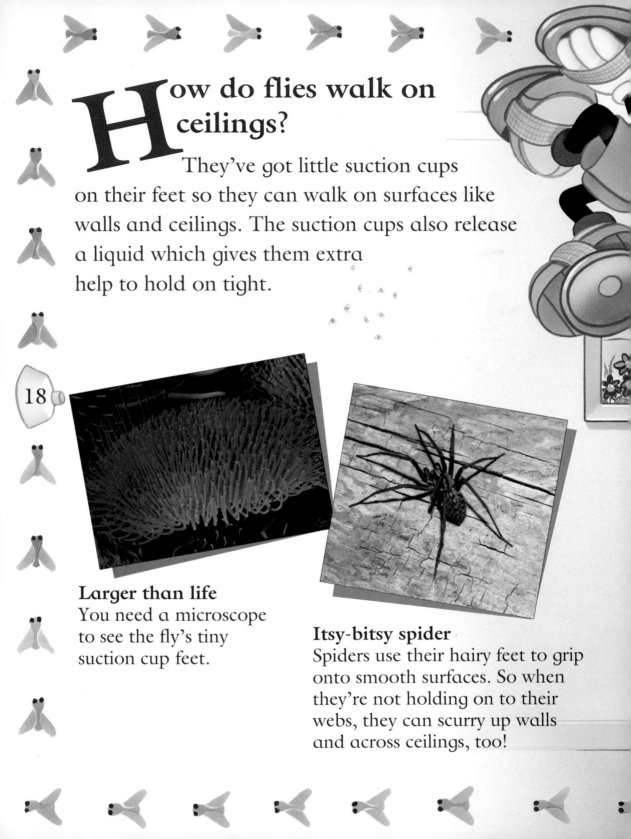

Larger than life
You need a microscope to see the fly's tiny suction cup feet.

Itsy-bitsy spider
Spiders use their hairy feet to grip onto smooth surfaces. So when they're not holding on to their webs, they can scurry up walls and across ceilings, too!

No flies on me!

☞ Flies can "taste" sugar through their feet, because they have taste buds on their toes!

☞ Houseflies beat their wings 200 times per second. How exhausting!

Don't try it!
Even if you had suction cups on your feet, you'd be too heavy to hang upside down from the ceiling!

19

How do snakes move without legs?

They move their bodies in four different ways. Some wriggle along, pushing against stones and sticks. Some creep forward, using the scales on their bellies to grip the ground. Some bunch up and straighten out like an accordion, and some sneaky snakes slip along sideways.

Snakes in the air!

When it isn't resting, this snake flies through the air. That's because it's a flying snake! It pushes out its ribs and pulls in its belly until it is flat like a ribbon. Then it leaps into the air and glides from tree to tree.

Slithering times

👉 Garter snakes and pythons move very slowly. It takes them at least an hour to travel one mile.

👉 The fastest snake is the black mamba from Africa, which can travel seven miles in one hour.

How do starfish move?

They scurry around the sea on hundreds of tiny feet, called tubefeet, which are found underneath their five arms. Starfish are pretty, but not very smart. They have no head, no brain, and an eye at the end of each arm.

Fancy footwork
Here are the starfish's feet. Each little foot has a suction cup at the end. The cups grab onto a surface and hold on tight!

Crown-of-thorns starfish
These large, spiky starfish are covered with sharp, poisonous spines. They eat living coral.

The amazing starfish

☞ If a starfish loses an arm, a new one will grow back. If a starfish gets cut in half, each half grows new arms and soon you've got two starfish.

☞ Most starfish have five arms but the sun starfish has twelve.

Why do kangaroos hop?

Because they can't run or walk! Their legs are made just for hopping. Their big back legs have thick strong bones and muscles, so jumping is easy. They can hop along for miles and miles without getting tired or out of breath.

In the pouch!
When they are born, baby kangaroos are about the size of a bean. Mother kangaroos keep their babies in a special pouch. The babies stay there and feed on Mom's milk until they are big and strong.

Hop to it!

☞ When people from Europe first went to Australia they were amazed by the sight of kangaroos. They asked a native Australian what these funny animals were called. They were told "kan ga roo." This means "I don't understand" in the Aborigine language.

Time for lunch
Kangaroos eat only leaves and grasses. They are vegetarians.

How do snails move?

They creep along using the big muscular foot underneath their body. The muscles in this foot move like a wave, pushing the snail forward.

Thick slime

The snail lays down a trail of slime, like a slippery carpet, to make sure it doesn't hurt itself on sharp stones. Its slimy trail works so well that it could crawl along the edge of a razor blade without being cut.

What's a slug?

It's a snail without a shell!

26

Slithery slimy facts

☞ Snails hide away during the wintertime. During this time, they seal the entrance to their shell shut.

☞ Some snails have 150,000 tiny teeth on their tongues. These are very helpful because snails like to munch on plants.

☞ The biggest land snail is the African land snail, which is eight inches long.

MICKEY'S Mind teaser

Look underneath each row to find the missing piece to complete each animal picture.

Can you remember the names of these animals?

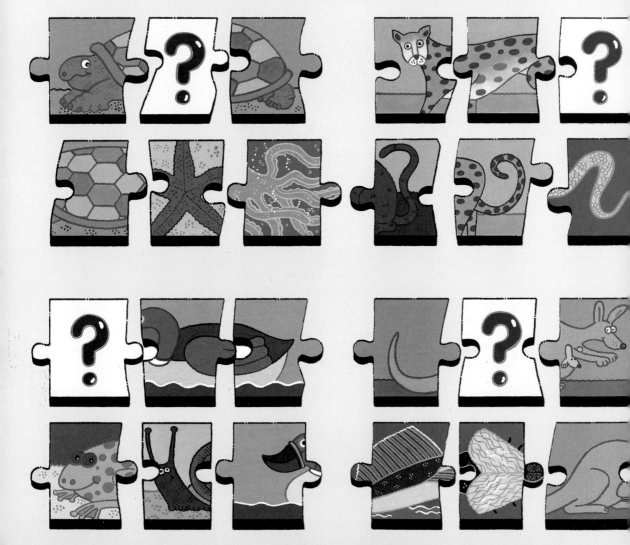